Best of
Both Worlds

Best of Both Worlds

Iris Howden

Published in association with
The Basic Skills Agency

Hodder & Stoughton
A MEMBER OF THE HODDER HEADLINE GROUP

Acknowledgements
Illustrations: Jim Eldridge.
Cover: Ben Warner/Organisation.

Orders: please contact Bookpoint Ltd, 39 Milton Park, Abingdon, Oxon OX14
4TD. Telephone: (44) 01235 400414, Fax: (44) 01235 400454. Lines are open
from 9.00–6.00, Monday to Saturday, with a 24 hour message answering service.
Email address: orders@bookpoint.co.uk

British Library Cataloguing in Publication Data
A catalogue record is available from The British Library

ISBN 0 340 72095 6

First published 1998
Impression number 10 9 8 7 6 5 4 3 2
Year   2002 2001 2000 1999

Typeset by Fakenham Photosetting Limited, Fakenham, Norfolk NR21 8NL
Printed in Great Britain for Hodder & Stoughton Educational, a division of
Hodder Headline Plc, 338 Euston Road, London NW1 3BH by Athenaeum Press
Ltd, Gateshead, Tyne & Wear.

Best of Both Worlds

Contents

1

A Letter

The letter had a London post mark.
'Go on,' Su's mum said. 'Open it.
I bet you've got an interview.'
Su tore open the envelope.
The letter was typed.
It asked her to go for an interview
the next Tuesday.

Su wanted to be a nanny.
She had taken a course in child care
at the local college.
Now she was looking for a job.
She had written off to adverts in the paper.
This was her first reply.

'I'm not sure,' Su told her mum.
'London's a long way from home.'
'Don't be silly,' her mum said.
'It's what you want – to be a nanny.
You'll have to get over being so shy.'

Su's full name was Su-ling Harris.
Her mother was Chinese.
Her father was English.
At school, Su-ling felt different from
the other girls.
Her family ate different food.
Her mum wore different clothes.

Su once tried to talk about it
with her dad, but he got angry.
He loved her mum very much.
'What's the matter Su?' he asked.
'Are you ashamed of your mum?'
'No, of course not,' Su said.
'It's just that people at school say things.'
'What sort of things?' her dad asked.
Su couldn't tell him.
She knew he would be hurt.

'Take no notice,' her dad told her.
'You were born here. You're English.'
But Su didn't always feel English.
The trouble was, she didn't feel Chinese either.
Su had her mother's dark eyes
but her father's brown wavy hair.
She was taller than a Chinese girl would be.
Her little brother Tommy looked Chinese.
Su felt neither one thing nor the other.

She could not even speak Chinese.
Her mum always spoke English to them.
She spoke English quite well
but she could not write it.
When her dad was away on a trip,
Su had to help her mum write notes
to Tommy's teacher if he was ill.
She helped her mum fill in forms.
'You're a good girl,' her mum told her.
'I shall miss you when you leave home.'

On the day of the interview, Su set off early.
She had to find her way across London.
Her mum had made her a new dress to wear.
She had given her the train fare.
'Good luck, Su,' she said. 'Do your best.'

The house was very grand.
It had a lovely garden.
Two smart cars were parked in the drive.
They must be a very rich family.

Tom and Jenny Morgan made her feel
at ease. They gave her a cup of tea.
Then they asked her questions.
They asked her about herself and her family.
They also asked about the course she had done
and why she wanted the job.

'I love children,' Su told them.
'And I'm used to looking after
my little brother.' When she talked
about Tommy she forgot to be shy.
'I'm sure I could do the job,' she said.
Then they brought the children in.
Becky was four and Tim was two.
Su liked them at once.
They seemed to take to her.
Soon the three of them were playing
with toys on the floor.
'I don't think we need look any further,'
Tom told his wife.
Su-ling had got the job.

2

Life in London

At first, Su found her new life strange.
She had never been away from home before.
She had always lived in a small town.
Tom and Jenny were very kind to her.
Su had her own room and her own TV set.
She had plenty of free time.

Later, when she met other nannies,
she found out how lucky she was.

Some of them had no free time.
They had to do lots of housework.
One girl was always hungry.
She never had enough to eat.
Some of the children they looked after
were very spoiled.
Su was pleased that Becky and Tim
were such nice children.

The family had a good life style.
Tom had a job in advertising.
He made a lot of money.
Jenny worked for a charity called CHILD AID.
They had lots of smart friends,
good clothes, a lovely home.
They went out quite a bit, but Jenny
made sure Su had some evenings free.

One of the other nannies, Greta,
a Dutch girl, took her to join a club.
People from different countries met there.
Some were nannies like Su.
Some worked in hotels. Some were students.

At one of these evenings she met Liang.

Liang was a student from China.

He was at a language school for a year.

He wanted to learn English.

'You speak it very well,' Su-ling told him.

'I don't know a word of Chinese
even though my mother was born in China.'

'There are many different languages
in China,' Liang told her.

'It's a huge country.

Where is your mother from?'

'She came from Yangshou,' Su-ling said.

'But the family moved to Hong Kong.

That's where she met my dad.'

'Yangshou is a very pretty place,' Liang said.

'On the banks of a great river.

There are hills there with strange names:

Horse hill, Crab hill, Lion hill and so on.'

'I come from Beijing. That's the capital.
It's a big modern city but you can still see
the old part.
It's called "The Forbidden City".
That's where the emperors of China lived.
Do you know London well?
Perhaps you could show me around.'
Su-ling had to admit that she did not
know London at all.
'I come from a small town
in the north,' she said.
'Well, we can explore together,' Liang said.

Over the next few weeks
they went sight-seeing.
They saw the Tower of London
and Buckingham Palace.
They went to the museums and parks.
They went down the River Thames on a boat.

They took the open-topped bus
around the city.
Su felt as though her life was just beginning.
There was so much to see.

She told Tom and Jenny about Liang.
They asked him to tea one Sunday.
Su knew they wanted to check on him.
To make sure he was OK.
'He's very nice,' Jenny said the next day.
'I'm sure your parents would like him.'

Su began to wonder if this was true.
Liang made China seem real to her.
He made her see that there was part
of herself she knew nothing about.
He made her want to know more.

Her dad had always told her
she was English.
He always called her Su.
Now Liang began to call her Su-ling.
'It's such a pretty name,' he said.
'Why not use it?'

3

A Holiday in Italy

The family were going on holiday.
Jenny had booked a villa in Italy.
They would be there for two weeks.
'You'll love it,' she told Su.
'It's a pretty spot, out in the country.
We'll fly to Pisa and get a hire car.'
Su was not so sure. She had never
flown before. Never been abroad.
She would miss London – and Liang.

'But you must go,' Liang told her.
'You can't let Tom and Jenny down.
And it's a great chance for you.
Staying in Italy, seeing all the sights.
All that sunshine, Italian food.
Don't worry, I'll still be here
when you get back.'

The family took a plane to Italy.
They flew over some mountains.
'Those are the Alps below us,' Tom said.
'Look, there's still snow on top of them.'
Su looked out of the window.
She forgot to be scared. It felt strange.
To be flying high above the clouds.

When Su got off the plane
the heat hit her at once.
She and Jenny piled their bags
on to a trolley.
They waited while Tom hired a car.

There was a two hour drive ahead of them.
At first things did not look very different.
They were on a motorway, in fast traffic.

Soon they were out in the country.
They drove down dusty roads with fields
on each side.
People were out working, cutting plants.
'That's tobacco,' Jenny told her.
'And look, a field of sunflowers.
They grow those for their oil.'
On the hillsides, vines grew in neat rows.
'This area's well known for its red wine,'
Tom said. 'We'll take some back with us.'

They got to the villa by late afternoon.
The stone house had once been a farm.
Now it was a smart holiday home.
There was a swimming pool and
a large patio with a table and chairs.
'Oh good, there's a barbecue,' Tom said.
'What do you say to a meal outside?'

They sorted out the bedrooms.
Su bathed the children and put them to bed.
They were tired after the long journey.
Then she and Tom and Jenny sat outside.
Drinking wine. Eating steak and salad.
It was a lovely evening.
The air was warm and
filled with a sweet scent.

Su was glad she had come.
It was all so new to her.
Sitting out on the patio
with a glass of wine in her hand.
On her first holiday abroad.

The first week passed quickly.
Sometimes they all went out together.
Sometimes Tom and Jenny went alone.
They left Su in charge.
The children often had a nap
in the afternoon.

Su had a lot of time on her hands.
There was a maid to do the housework.
Su swam in the pool or sat in the sun.
She wrote postcards home.
'Having a great time,' she wrote to Liang.
'It's hot and sunny. There's lots to see.
We've been to Sienna for the day.'

Sometimes she drew in her sketch book.
She tried to draw the villa.
The green hills with their spiky poplar trees.
At other times she made sketches of clothes.
Su's mother could make up any style
from a sketch.
She had been a machinist in Hong Kong.

Before coming to Italy, Jenny had given
Su time off to visit her family.
'I'll need some clothes for the evenings,'
she told her mum.
'Tom and Jenny go to such smart places.'
'I'll make you one or two outfits,'
her mum said. 'What did you have in mind?'

Jenny showed her the sketches she'd made.

'But these are Chinese styles,' her mum said.

She sounded surprised.

Su didn't tell her that they were Liang's idea.

'You'd look good in Chinese dress,' he'd said.

'I'll see what I can do,' her mum said.

She worked very quickly.

She found some rolls of silk Su's dad

had brought back from his travels.

Soon Su had some pretty new outfits

to take on holiday

Su soon got the chance to wear them.

4

House Guests

Guests were coming to stay.

There was an older woman called Chris.

She worked with Jenny at CHILD AID.

The other woman was Tom's boss, Zara.

She was bringing her two children.

Tom went to fetch them from the airport.

'You'll like Chris,' Jenny told her.
'She's a lovely person. So kind.
I don't know Zara all that well.
She's had a bad time lately.
She and her husband have split up.'
Jenny didn't say any more. Su got the idea
she didn't like Zara very much.

Su hated her on sight.
As soon as she arrived she started
bossing her around.
'Are you the nanny?
Take the children upstairs
and tidy them up. I need a rest.'
She treated Su like a servant.

Jenny had a word with Su later.
'Don't get upset,' she said. 'Do you think
you can manage four children?'
'Of course,' Su told her.
She was a trained nanny.
She would do her best.

It was not easy.
Zara's children, Sophie and James
were very spoiled.
They did not play like Becky and Tim.
They didn't take care of their toys.
They would shout and scream if they
did not get all their own way.
Su found them very hard work.

Zara was even worse. She spoke about Su
as though she wasn't there.
'These girls are all the same,' she said.
'No idea most of them.
I've had dozens of nannies.'
'We're very lucky to have Su,' Jenny said.
'She's like one of the family.'

Zara was a snob.
Everything she had cost a lot.
The children wore designer clothes.
They even had designer sun glasses.

'Of course you have to pay for the best,'
Zara said one day.
'These shorts I have on cost the earth.
But they're worth the money.
You don't get the cut in cheap clothes.'
She was looking at Su's shorts as she said it.

Then Chris spoke up.
'When you're young and pretty like Su
you don't need designer clothes,' she said.
'It's only when we get older that
we need to spend money to look good.'
'I'm sorry my dear,' she said to Jenny later.
'I know she's Tom's boss, but I couldn't
let that woman get away with it.
She's a real bitch!'

That evening they were going out to eat.
Two taxis came to take them to the restaurant.

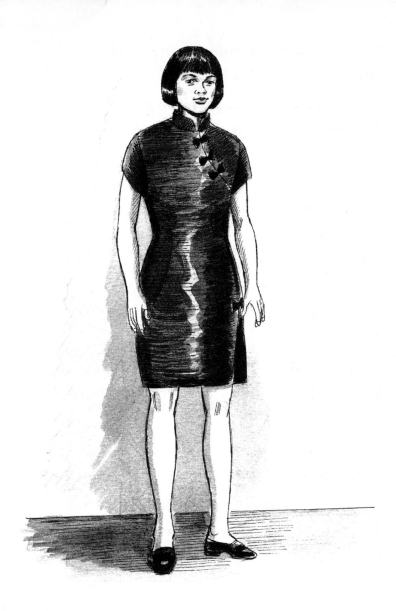

Su spent a lot of time getting ready.
She wore one of her new dresses.
She tied her hair back in a long plait.
Put on the jade ear rings
her parents had given her for her 18th.

'You look lovely,' Chris said when she
came in.
'Doesn't she Jenny?'
'Really nice,' Jenny agreed.
'I love the dress. Is it new?'
'Yes, it's one my mum made for me,' Su said.
'You look like a real Chinese lady now,'
Becky said.

This made Su laugh.
'Then you'll have to call me
by my Chinese name,' she said.
'I'm Su-ling, not Su, tonight.'

5

A Fashion Show

Next day Tom, Jenny and Zara went out.
The others stayed at the villa.
The children had a nap after their late night.
Chris was tired too.
'I can't face any more old churches,' she said.
'You three go. I shall stay with Su.'
They sat on the patio with a jug
of iced lemon drink.
'This is nice,' Chris said.

She read her book for a while.

Su made sketches on her pad.

'What are those?' Chris asked.

'Designs for clothes. For Becky's doll,'
Su told her. 'I'll send them to my mum.
She'll make them up for Becky's birthday.'

'Let me look,' Chris said. 'They're good.
You've quite a talent for design.
Have you thought of taking a course?'
Su shook her head.

'Not really. I can't draw well enough,' she said.
'It's just a hobby. I love my job.'

'They've given me an idea,' Chris said.
'Jenny and I want to raise funds
for CHILD AID.

We could put on a fashion show – for children.
These designs would make lovely kids' clothes.
I can just see Becky in that sun dress.
And the little trouser suit would look great
on a Chinese child.

We could get children of different races
to model them.'

Back in London, Chris had the clothes made up.
The big chain stores lent them other outfits.
The show would be in a top London hotel.
It would make a lot of money for CHILD AID.

On the night, Su and Liang had seats
in the front row.
The children came down the cat walk in pairs.
They walked hand in hand.
People clapped the little models.
They looked so sweet.

Becky came on with Amy, her Chinese
friend from play group.
They stole the show.
Flash bulbs went off all around them.
All the photographers took pictures of them.

Next morning they were on the front page
of every newspaper.
EAST MEETS WEST one headline said.
The phone never stopped ringing.

Jenny was really pleased.

All this publicity was good for CHILD AID.

It meant more cash for the charity.

'Your designs are a real hit,' she told Su.

'One of the magazines is sending
a reporter round.

They want to interview you.'

6

Home for a Visit

Next time Su went home on a visit
her father was there.
She had not seen him for a year.
He had been away at sea.
He was very tanned and fit.
Su gave him a hug.
'Hi, dad,' she said. 'You look great.'
'So do you,' he said. 'So grown up.
How's London?'

'Fantastic,' Su said. 'I really love it.
And I love my job.
Tom and Jenny are really good to me.
The children are nice too.'
She had so much to tell him.
About her trip to Italy.
About the fashion show.
She showed her parents
the photos from the papers.

Then she got out the magazine.
She'd been saving this till last.
In it was the article with her photo.
SU-LING SETS THE STYLE FOR TOTS,
the headline said.
It went on to say how her Chinese-style
clothes had been the hit of the show.
'One or two firms making children's wear
have shown an interest in Su-ling's designs,'
the article said.
'But the young nanny prefers to keep on
her job with a London family.'

'Fame at last,' her dad teased her.

'But I'm really pleased for you.

What's all the sudden interest in China?'

he asked.

Su took a deep breath.

It was time to tell her parents about Liang.

'He's a really nice person,' she said.

'Tom and Jenny have met him.

They like him a lot.'

'It's your choice,' her dad said.

He put his arm round her mum.

'I made mine and I don't regret it.

Is it serious then?'

Su nodded. 'What if I go to live in China?'

'Then we'll come and visit you,' her dad said.

'We only want you to be happy, Su.

As happy as we've been.'

'Liang has to go home soon,' Su said.
'His course ends this month.
He wants to work in radio or TV in China.
So he may get the chance to come
back to London from time to time.
I'm saving up to visit him in Beijing.
I've got the fee the magazine paid me.
And I may sell more of my designs.'

'Mum, I want you to help me learn
some words of Chinese before I go.
And dad could give me some tips
for when I travel.'
They stayed up late talking.
Su felt very close to her parents.
Now her own life was turning out
so well. She was happy.
She had the best of both worlds.

LIVEWIRE YOUTH FICTION